The author
teaching classical dance to
her seventh term girls.

THE BOLSHOI
BALLET SCHOOL

This book is made possible through the courtesy of VAAP, the copyright agency of the Soviet Union. The publishers would like to express their thanks to VAAP and its administrators for making this project a successful example of the fruits of cooperation. All foreign language rights to this book are the property of T.F.H. Publications, Inc.

Design, layout, captions and cover by Dr. Herbert R. Axelrod.

The Bolshoi School prepares their own costumes. They are well made and very colorful as you can see.

Distributed in the UNITED STATES by T.F.H. Publications, Inc., 211 West Sylvania Avenue, Neptune City, NJ 07753; in CANADA to the Book Trade by Macmillan of Canada (A Division of Canada Publishing Corporation), 164 Commander Boulevard, Agincourt, Ontario M1S 3C7; in ENGLAND by T.F.H. Publications Limited, 4 Kier Park, Ascot, Berkshire SL5 7DS; in AUSTRALIA AND THE SOUTH PACIFIC by T.F.H. (Australia) Pty. Ltd., Box 149, Brookvale 2100 N.S.W., Australia; in NEW ZEALAND by Ross Haines & Son, Ltd., 18 Monmouth Street, Grey Lynn, Auckland 2 New Zealand; in SINGAPORE AND MALAYSIA by MPH Distributors (S) Pte., Ltd., 601 Sims Drive, #03/07/21, Singapore 1438; in the PHILIPPINES by Bio-Research, 5 Lippay Street, San Lorenzo Village, Makati Rizal; in SOUTH AFRICA by Multipet Pty. Ltd., 30 Turners Avenue, Durban 4001. Published by T.F.H. Publications Inc. Manufactured in the United States of America by T.F.H. Publications, Inc.

THE BOLSHOI BALLET SCHOOL

*Student Life in
the World's Most Prestigious Dance School*

By Sophia N. Golovkina

*Translated by Nigel Timothy Coey;
Photos by Vladimir Pcholkin, Moscow.*

Foreword

People's Artist Sophia Golovkina, a State Prize holder, is one of the all-time greats of the Soviet choreographic school. She was a Bolshoi ballet star in the thirties, forties and fifties and has since taught and directed at the Moscow Academy Choreographic School.

Sophia Golovkina graduated from the Moscow Choreographic School in 1933, being accepted from A.I. Chekrygin's class directly into the Bolshoi Ballet. She stood out for her rare sense of purpose, energy and constant efforts to refine her style. Her dancing demonstrated daring, confidence, elegance and vitality. She was perfect technique incarnate. Yet the dancer was never content with her professional skill and was always looking for more expression in her performances. She was often seen at the drama theater, especially the Moscow Arts Theatre. She knew V.I. Nemirovich-Danchenko and other luminaries and chatted long with them to gain insight into their art. From the Moscow Arts Theater she learned drama.

The ballerina handled dramatic and comedic roles with equal aplomb. Her many dancing successes included Nikiya in Ludwig Minkus's "La Bayadère," the Princess in Cesare Pugni's "The Little Humpbacked Horse," Raymonda in A. Glazunov's ballet, Swanilda in L. Delibe's "Coppelia," Zarema in B. Asafiev's "The Fountain of Bachisarai," Paracha in R. Gliere's "The Bronze Horseman" and roles in the Tchaikovsky ballets "The Sleeping Beauty," "The Nutcracker" and "Swan Lake." For her portrayal of Diane Mirelle in Asafiev's "The Flame of Paris" Sophia Golovkina was awarded the USSR State Prize.

During World War II, or the "Great Patriotic War" as Soviet people remember the years of 1941-5, Sophia Golovkina was among the Bolshoi Ballet stars who remained in Moscow: she performed at the Bolshoi's second theater and in factories. In the time left over after performances and rehearsals she worked with her countrymen at the defense lines, extinguished incendiary bombs on the roofs of buildings, stood watch in hospitals, and was a blood donor to the war-wounded.

Since 1960, Sophia Nikolaevna Golovkina, as Director and a teacher of classical dance at the Moscow Academy Choreographic School, has been passing on her vast experience and artistic vision to budding new stars.

"I made up my mind to stop performing but not to end my involvement with ballet," says Sophia Golovkina. "With that began a second life for me. I went back to the old school to pursue my work through my students and their dancing . . ."

Back at the School, Sophia Golovkina showed herself to be a fine organizer with a quick and inquisitive mind. It was difficult taking over the whole administrative set-up, supervising the erection of a new School building and dealing with a business side that often seemed remote from ballet.

Today the Moscow Academy Choreographic School is the Soviet Union's leading institution of its kind, an educational center for choreographic training. The teaching staff under Sophia Golovkina have worked out new curricula for special disciplines and two-year courses for choreographic teachers have been organized. The School has also produced educational films and aids for classical and folk dance.

Sophia Golovkina has won world fame as a prima ballerina, a brilliant dancer with exquisite technique. Her lessons reflect her dancing: They are full of liveliness and expression, combining artistic freedom with study bases. Sophia Golovkina the teacher senses the theater of today, and today's more complex technique which demands from the performer complete coordination, stamina and artistry. Hence the School's graduates are equipped with excellent knowledge and a strong professional grounding, which means that when they join the company they quickly adapt and are able to take on the most difficult of solo parts.

Many of her students have won Soviet and international competitions and have been critically acclaimed. They include USSR People's Artist Natalya Bessmertnova, Russian People's Artist Nina Sorokina, Merited Russian Artist Marina Leonova and Merited Uzbek Artist Alla Mikhalchenko.

She has initiated the revival of many ballets and sponsored short ballets by young choreographers. The School works well with the Bolshoi Theater.

Sophia Golovkina is to be seen every day at the School, and is known to be strict, full of vigor, and to demand artistic discipline. Teacher, mentor and artist, she is totally dedicated to choreography and is doing her utmost to enable future generations of Soviet ballet stars to continue the work which her generation has begun.

Y.N. GRIGOROVICH

By
Sophia N.
Golovkina

The Moscow Choreographic School is my life. Everything I have done is connected to it. There I once began my career, just as my pupils are beginning theirs. I entered the school of ballet in 1926 and graduated in 1933 when the Bolshoi Ballet took me on to dance solo.

My teachers were the excellent A. Chekrygin, V. Semyonov, A. Monakhov and E. Gerdt. A. Vaganskaya refined my technique. I have danced with such greats as M. Semyonova, A. Ermolaev, A. Messerere and A. Rudenko, and under ballet masters such as F. Lopuchov, L. Lavrovksy, R. Zacharov and V. Vainonen.

I have had the great happiness to dance the leading roles of "Swan Lake," "Sleeping Beauty," "Don Quixote," "Raymonda" and "La Bayadere" at the Bolshoi. Twenty-seven years of professional dancing just flew past.

In 1960 I returned to my old school to become its Director and a teacher of classical dance.

To be offered the position was at once a real honor and major responsibility. The Moscow School is one of our country's oldest institutions. It dates back to 1773, the year "dance classes" were introduced at the home for orphans and the children of the poor. At that time there were 26 girls and 28 boys.

Over two hundred years have elapsed and many eminent dancers have emerged from the Moscow School to write new pages in the history of Russian and Soviet ballet.

E. Geltser and M. Mordkin, A. Messerere and M. Gabovich, I. Moiseev and T. Ustinova, M. Plisetskaya and M. Liepa, V. Vasiliev and E. Maksimova, N. Bessmertnova and M. Lavrovsky, I. Mukhammedov and V. Gordeev, A. Mikhalchenko and G. Taranda are among a host of names that have become famous internationally.

So the Moscow School has gained world renown. Naturally, it is associated with the Bolshoi Ballet having for two centuries produced new blood for it. But in addition graduates give us links with all our other national ballet companies.

Interest in ballet is immense in this country of 60 opera and ballet theaters which are always looking for fresh young talent.

The Moscow School gives a good, sound grounding in ballet choreography. It and the St. Petersburg School were the only schools of their kind before the Revolution. Today there are twenty schools of which our Moscow School is the premier.

By the early sixties the Moscow School badly needed a new location, as the old 19th century building could no longer satisfy growing requirements. By 1967 the new building was built and opened.

The contemporary Moscow Choreographic School is a palace of ballet and dance. A fine 3-story building with a shaded garden, it is located in the city center on the banks of the Moscow River. Here, a student will find all that he needs to become a professional dancer.

We have 600 students. Of them 300 are in the boarding section, which receives children from outside Moscow and from abroad. The dormitories are bright and comfortable.

Each spring we open the doors for hundreds of boys and girls from all over our country who dream of a career in dance. There are lot of applicants, more than 20 per place. We accept 90 children, 45 boys and 45 girls, every year. They are ten years old when they come to us after a three-stage entrance examination. At the first stage, physique and body proportions are checked. Those who pass through to the second stage undergo a rigorous medical examination. At the third stage, a panel of experienced teachers judges the suitability of the children for ballet: their dancing, expression, feel for music and coordination.

Ours is a nation of song and dance. Just about every school student participates in singing or dancing, gymnastics or ice skating classes. And children are taught from kindergarten age to dance and sing in their own amateur productions.

Recent years have seen the School largely filled by children with some dance training from dance groups, or gymnastics lessons. The School has a one-year evening preparatory department with classes three times a week. And our teaching staff travels the country in search of talent.

We see our mission as not to train just highly professional ballet dancers but also people of artistic bent capable of creating and working independently.

Studies at our school can be divided into three subject ranges. Our students go through a general secondary education that covers language and literature, mathematics, physics, chemistry and so on. This education is identical to that received by all children in the USSR.

To learn the skills a ballet dancer needs we give special courses in Classical, Duet, Character, Historic and Modern dancing as well as in acting. Our pupils take seven years of music school piano forte classes. Then there are various art subjects—history of ballet, theater and the arts, and esthetics. We try to give the student just the right blend. We think that's what makes an exceptional dancer.

The School is a huge place with 20 large bright dance halls. One wall is all mirror, the opposite all windowglass. The floor is made of the best pine, the kind of which ships were once made. It absorbs shock well, which is most vital for developing jumping technique.

There are 20 music rooms at the School and each pupil has individual lessons.

The lecture halls and science classrooms etc., have all the modern equipment and teaching aids. We have a gymnasium, canteen, photo lab, costumer's and a medical clinic with a good range of specialists.

We have over 300 people on our staff, all of whom are highly proficient, first-rate former dancers from the Bolshoi and other national ballet companies.

Many of them have had special courses in teaching. All are very eager to pass on their knowledge and experience. P. Pestov, N. Zolotova, A. Prokofiev, G. Kuznetsova, L. Zhdanov, L. Litavkina, E. Malakhovskaya, L. Nikonova and B. Rachmanin have produced a great many talents. Our teaching staff all live and breathe dance. They love the pupils and are really interested in them. We exert a great deal of effort to bring out our students' capabilities. We try, beyond teaching dance, to promote individual style.

Classes keep to a gruelling timetable from 9 a.m. to 6 p.m. We alternate the physical and mental aspects of education. After classical dance comes math, after duet, physics, after gymnastics, music.

The emphasis is on Classical Dance. From the first grade on there are daily one-and-a-half hour classes in it, girls and boys separately. As for every other dance subject, there is a special curriculum.

The curriculum is broken down into each year. The degree of difficulty is gradually increased, the pupils proceeding in dance technique from simple to more complex movement. Classical dance makes the ballet dancer versatile. It promotes harmonious development of the dancer, instills coordination of movement, expression, stamina and technique. The classical dance is a stepping stone to success in any contemporary style of dance.

In the first and second grades Historic and Modern Dance studies begin and are continued in the sixth year of attendance. The children learn dances of different eras and style—quadrille, polonaise, minuet, sarabande, foxtrot, waltz, etc., along with contemporary ballroom dances.

From the fourth to the finishing grades we teach Character Dance, something we consider most important. The study of Hungarian, Russian, Spanish, Italian, Ukrainian, Polish and other national and folk dances lets the students flower and prepares them for the diverse life of the theater. We try to get across the style and character of the dance as well as the technique. We especially highlight the dances that are in the current theater repertoires.

One of the fortes of the Soviet school of dance has been that is has always managed to maintain the best traditions of our classical heritage while keeping apace of contemporary ballet repertoires. The twentieth century has brought a rhythm and flexibility all its own. The store of movements of the more modern trends in the dance arts are broadly used by the contemporary ballet-master. We have found jazz-dance lessons indispensable in giving insight into jazz music and contemporary movement, instilling a sense of rhythm and a special coordination that distinguishes it from classical dance. Our students love jazz-dance; they're caught up in it and feel free to improvise. Incidentally, we have noticed that jazz-dance has a favorable influence on the students' classical dance performance, making it more vivid and increasing the emotional charge.

In the last three years of study, the finishing classes, there appear on the curriculum, duet dance and acting. There isn't a ballet that hasn't a duet dance. What splendid adagios we see in the ballets "Swan Lake," "The Sleeping Beauty," "Giselle," "Spartacus" and "Chopiniana" among others. Many of these have become part of the history of dance. This is what makes the duet dance so important. We start teaching it when the student is 15 and 16 years old and should be physically and professionally geared to it. At duet classes the students first learn the technique before proceeding to short etudes prepared by the instructor. In the final year of study, the adagios from classical and contemporary theater repertoires are taught.

An artistic image can be produced only if the performer has a flowing proficiency as both dancer and actor. This comes after acting classes. These lessons teach the students to tackle roles with the Stanislavsky acting system principles. Much attention is attached to the dramatic content of the music. The students work to give an actor's image purely through dancing at first in etudes, and eventually by studying scenes from ballets. They just love the acting classes. This is the big chance to innovate, to portray a character, to convey a frame of mind, to play a scene—to become someone else.

Special gymnastics classes help the pupils a lot by developing professional attributes such as the step, jumping and twisting ability, and general flexibility. the classes start from the first grade, with the instructors and classical dance teachers interacting.

We also offer rhythmic movement classes to music, breathing exercises and makeup studies.

The musical education of our budding artists is very important. We have to teach them to listen to the music and catch, beyond the underlying rhythm, the mood, the content and the delicacy of the nuances. And, most important of all, all this has to be conveyed in dance with a maximum of expression in the performance.

The musical portion of the studies extends beyond the piano and music literature classes into the classical dance, national and folk, and duet lessons and other specialized subject disciplines.

The success of a teacher depends largely on close contact with the musical director. We need him to show great imagination in selecting music to fit the curriculum and the different flexibility elements required of boys and girls.

Each lesson always includes Russian and foreign classics and fine examples of progressive Soviet and foreign contemporary music. The music to a great extent brings out the individual style of the student, develops emotional qualities and reveals capacity for innovation.

Choreographic education means more than just churning out professional dancers. We seek to produce people who are highly educated and cultured, thinking artists.

The complex psychological characters in modern ballet such as Ivan the Terrible, Spartacus, Romeo and Juliet, and Til Eulenspiel demand of actors a thorough knowledge of history, literature as well as the history of theater, ballet, music and the fine arts.

We give each of these subjects the most painstaking attention.

Stage practice is vital for up-and-coming ballet dancers. This subject is rightly seen as the polish to all our special dance training work at the School.

From the very first grade these lessons have the children learning dance routines and scenes from the ballets. The movements they master in the morning at classes they put into stage form in the evening rehearsals. This means the students are taught to get used to rehearsing from a very early age and their artistry is born and developed. This is the vital, all-important progression from classroom to stage.

We hold practice performances three or four times a year. The repertoire comes from the classical heritage, more modern choreographers and national dances.

We have a special programme of pieces for each year of study.

We encourage and are proud of the efforts of our ballet-masters. Many of them compose lovely ballet etudes to melodic music specially selected together with the music director. Such etudes are built around movements already mastered by the students, only this time they are put into the art form.

It is a rule with us for all students to be involved in stage practice. By creating dance etudes the teacher is able to involve the whole class at once. The best students are given larger roles. The selections can be character as well as classical dance. Many pieces born in such a way have become repertoire and are included in the graduation Concerts.

The children's pas de trois from "The Nutcracker" in V. Vainonen's version is always a great hit. The most gifted third and fourth graders are assigned to it. M. Martirosian has produced a great many excellent dances for students of all age groups: solos and duets and group dances involving all the grades. And our students just love to dance modern. We arrange special stage compositions for 50 dancers at a time. And don't eleven-year-olds enjoy contemporary dancing to good modern music!

Our students receive invitations to take part in gala concerts in Moscow's biggest theater halls. The success they find there seems to give them the ability to handle the rigorous routines back at the School.

Our long-established ties with the Bolshoi Theater have a great deal to do with fostering young talent. From an early age the School's pupils are to be seen on the stage of the Bolshoi Theater and the Stanislavsky-Nemirovich-Danchenko Music Theater.

To appear in the ballets "The Sleeping Beauty" and "Don Quixote" in a world-famous theater alongside the ballet greats leaves an impression that will last a lifetime. It also gives the students a first taste of theatrical excitement. They hear the orchestra and see an audience. Oh, how crucial a step that is in the making of an artistic professional performer!

Many of the greatest ballet stars danced these children's parts in their school years. The current prima-ballerina at the Bolshoi, Natalya Bessmertnova, recalls with affection how she, as a third-grader, received the role of Amur in the dream scene in "Don Quixote" and first appeared at the Bolshoi. "It really was like a fairy-tale dream."

Fifteen years later little Alla Mikhalchenko, as Amur in "Don Quixote," with bated breath watched the brilliant Natalya Bessmertnova dance, and today as Amur a tiny girl called Nabokina watches with wide eyes as Alla Mikhalchenko dances Kitri. That is a memorable moment to treasure all one's days.

It is a longstanding tradition for the School's students to prepare whole ballets on their own. Established and budding ballet masters alike have worked with great energy with the students. In different times, ballets have been staged by K. Goleisovsky, V. Burmeister, N. Popko, O. Tarasova, L. Jacobson, V. Varkovitsky, A. Chichinadse and V. Vainonen, not to mention many others. The "Nutcracker" was performed by the School as early as 1933. It won a permanent place in the repertoire in V. Vainonen's setting in the fifties, as did A. Gorsky's "Vain Caution."

Of all the other ballets, I would like to note D. Klebanov's "Baby Stork," P. Tchaikovsky's "Snow Princess" and E. Krylatova's "The Seven-Flowering Flower."

L.M. Lavrovsky, the eminent Art Director at the School in the years 1964-7, contributed immense experience and talent. He placed great emphasis on stage practice, arranging several one-act ballets, such as Ravel's "Bolero" and "La Valse," and S. Prokofiev's "Classical Symphony" which has been in the School repertoire for over 20 years.

In 1949 A. Gorsky's ballet "Coppelia" was performed by the Bolshoi. It was a great pleasure for me to dance Swanilda alongside the fine A. Radunsky. It was a wonderful ballet but for some reason it was not in the repertoire for long. I dreamed of restoring it at our School.

In 1977 came the chance and we had a première.

The School Art Director M. Martirosian and I, along with A. Radunsky, produced a new script which kept the best of Gorsky's scores. We painstakingly rebuilt the pantomime "mise-en-scene"and wrote in a number of new children's dances, something vital for the School's youngest pupils.

The success of "Coppelia" surpassed all expectations. The show is frequently to be seen on the stage of the Kremlin Palace of Congresses which seats 6,000 and it is always sold out.

This inspired us to revamp "Vain Caution" (Gertel's music) on the same principles as "Coppelia." The première took place in the autumn of 1979. The ballet has become one of the great favorites of children, and indeed of adult audiences.

We see "Coppelia" and "Vain Caution" as the summit of stage practice at our School.

In May 1986 there was the première of "Timur and his Friends," children's ballet adapted from the novel of the same name by A. Gaidar with the arrangement by Andrei Petrov. Yuri Grigorovich, the principle ballet-master of the Bolshoi Theater, lent us invaluable assistance. He came to the rehearsals, gave advice, discussed decor and costumes, and helped us build up the dramatic line of the show. This keen interest in our quest and plans helped us to get off the ground. In the new ballet our students danced their roles with great fervor. Behind the stage after the performance, I found myself surrounded by the young members of the audience thanking us for the new ballet. They had liked it that much. It is moments like those that make everything worthwhile.

Our students adore performing in real ballets. For them they open up the intriguing and wonderful world of the theater.

For each and every one of them, mind you, it is a very responsible moment and they have their "butterflies"—the very first steps into the profession of ballet dancer.

Our shows have a lot of group dances, both classical and popular, where the pupils learn to perform harmoniously in company, holding to the complex theme of the dance and moving smoothly through the variations.

We allocate to the most gifted students the leading roles. More often than not, these students go on to solo roles in the theater proper.

To perform in such ballets demands laborious training day by day, week by week, month by month in the School's training rooms. The final performance is the result of study in all the specialized disciplines.

Our having such major shows in our repertoire definitely determines the course of our work. Each year students graduate, usually the performers of the leading roles, and those in the smaller parts are now a year older. This means that every year the cast has to be amended.

To find our new cast we arrange competitions for the leads, and indeed all the roles. The winners take the respective parts in the performance.

This constant renewal of the cast with new up-and-coming ballet dancers means the ballets don't grow stale. The shows retain their vitality and there is always a festive air about the première. Youthful ardor and directness come through.

I feel that a good tradition of ours is spending the two-month summer vacation on tour here or abroad. Our concerts show just what we have learned.

It is important that the students get to try themselves out as performers, sense the responsibility involved in their work, and experience the joy of communication with the audience. This is a crucial part of stage practice.

The School has toured many cities in the Soviet Union, and on more than one occasion. We've been to Leningrad, Ulyanovsk, Kishinev and so on, and even to Sakhalin and the Soviet Far East.

In the first foreign tour, back in the early fifties, the graduates of the School went to Prague and Berlin.

March 1961 saw eight graduates perform in the Italian city of Parma at the Eleventh International University Theater Festival.

Of our pupils who went on to become world famous, let me mention N. Bessmertnova, M. Lavrovsky and N. Sorokina.

In 1967 the School took part in the 5th International Ballet Festival in Paris as a hors de concours entry. Another really big success.

The "Aurora" correspondent wrote: "Hors de Concours Company Takes Grand Prix!"

The French daily "Le Monde" said: "What a vigorous and powerful onslaught! What grace and ability these young Russian dancers have on the stage!"

After France came England.

The "Evening News" said our young people had all the pure elegance, fine training and mathematical accuracy in movement and gesture that are the hallmark of the Russian school of ballet.

The "Daily Telegraph" said that not too many national companies were in a position to generate the pure pleasure received from watching the company with its simple, clean manner of performance, and beauty of style.

The summer of 1970 brought new foreign tours, this time to France, Italy, Monaco and Spain.

In 1973 for the first time the School went to the United States of America, performing alongside the Bolshoi Theater Company. We had 60 of our students in the group and we gave 27 concerts in a variety of American cities. We were very excited and put great care and effort into our performances. Our pupils were just great: so orderly and controlled. They performed every single piece with genuine inspiration.

Sol Hurok, that well-known impresario, wrote that a young offshoot of the Bolshoi Ballet had arrived to give second wind to Russian ballet's popularity. He said that today, when it was pretty hard to surprise anyone with anything, we had astounded. In the heat of the "off-season" we had produced an original oasis of freshness.

The "New York Post" correspondent, Francis Harridge, wrote that the Moscow Choreographic School student performance was the big hit of the program and was absolutely delightful.

A Washington critic wrote: "If you want to purge yourself, if you want your soul to come in touch with purity, beauty and directness, go and see this concert of the Bolshoi Ballet training school."

Of our more recent tours, the one to Japan in the summer of '85 stands out in my memory.

There were 75 of us, students (aged 16-20 years) and teachers. In 45 days we gave 25 concerts and were on all the Japanese islands. We showed our Japanese audiences the second act of Tchaikovsky's "Swan Lake," Gertel's "Vain Caution," Delibe's "Coppelia" and a big concert program to the music of our twentieth-century Soviet composers. We were endeavoring to render the classical heritage and at the same time more modern hits and the national and folk dances of our peoples.

We lived and worked among young folk. Our concerts were accompanied by a Japanese youth orchestra. They traveled with us from city to city and joined in our success. We soon became good friends.

Our performances required smaller children so we decided to invite Japanese children. We gathered the students of all the Tokyo ballet schools. Each child thought it a dream to dance with our Soviet students. How happy they were! How diligent and attentive! Before long we included them in our shows. Our Japanese audiences were surprised and delighted to see their young people perform.

The huge concert halls were full to bursting with children and after the performances they crowded round our young Soviet artists. And conversation started. Our children knew no Japanese, and the Japanese no Russian. Yet they momentarily found a common language—the language of friendship. They clung to each other, eager to find out more and more about each other.

The School does not accept only Moscow children. We have entrants from other cities and other Republics in our country in addition to some from abroad.

The first foreign students appeared at the School in the mid-fifties.

Now it is something of a tradition. In the past thirty years over 150 people from 50 countries have been trained or come on exchange visits to the Moscow Academy Choreographic School.

Apart from this, we have had young people arriving from all over the world for one to two year refinement courses. We have received students from Britain, France, the USA, Hungary, Poland, Romania, Mexico, Cuba, China, Chile and Albania among other countries. We have signed a two-way agreement with Italy's La Scala Theater. Now we have ballet students from the theater and its ballet studio with us. Our country is sending singers from national opera theaters to study at La Scala.

We also get ballet artists from other cities in Italy. Over recent years 50 Italian students have been guests of ours. They usually study beside our children at classes and parallel to this have special individual lessons with our coaches during which they prepare dance numbers from the ballet repertoire.

We accept upcoming ballet instructors as well as the young performers. Many of our foreign students and exchange visitors go on to become famous ballet masters, dancers and teachers. Magda Salek and Koldamova Krasimira later headed choreographic schools in Egypt and Bulgaria.

In 1982, after two years of study with us, Aromaa Iukka, a Finnish student, finished with honors. Two years later, Aromaa won an International Ballet Competition in her native land.

Bulgarian ballet dancers Noveva Diana and Spasov Borislav, recent graduates of our School, performed with credit in the summer of 1986 at the International Ballet Competition in Varna.

And there is no shortage of other such instances. At the 5th Moscow International

Ballet Contest, Argentinian dancer Julio Bokka rehearsed and trained at the School with our classical dance teacher Alexander Bondarenko.

After winning the Competition, Julio Bokka said that he had had a dream fulfilled in being able to perfect his skill at the Moscow Choreographic School. Well, we are always glad to welcome students wherever they come from in the world.

Our School is a training center for choreographic education. Programs are composed of special disciplines and backed up with teaching aids and a large amount of research work. We give out a great deal of advice and recommendations every year on matters related to choreographic training, and our instructors travel on a regular basis to other schools to give training and practical assistance.

At the end of each academic year there are examinations in all dance disciplines. The examination covers all the material in the curriculum for that year of training. In addition, a free program is presented to demonstrate artistic and dancing ability.

The instructor arranges the examination proceeding from his personal teaching and artistic experience in his capacity of ballet-master. This comes through especially vividly in the graduate examinations which look like real shows.

We also have teacher training courses at the School, offering a careful blend of theoretical study in the dance disciplines with practical classroom studies.

All of us, while striving to convey individuality in our work, have the same study plans and methods of teaching. The brighter and richer the personality of the teacher as a dancer, the more his students get out of the classes and the greater their artistic merit and taste.

While maintaining the traditions in teaching passed down by generations of Russian and Soviet teachers, we are utilizing innovations in our methods for developing professional dance technique. We inspect teaching methods the world over.

Our teaching staff goes to other lands to examine the system of choreographic education and the teaching methods employed; and teachers from other nations are frequent guests of ours. This kind of contact is extremely worthwhile. Our students have been given lessons in classical dance by the immortal Harald Lander and Ferdinando Alonso.

Not long ago, the great French ballerina Claude Bessy who now runs the ballet school of the Paris Opera, was at the School. She attended our lessons and rehearsals for a week and herself gave a number of demonstrations and told us of the ballet training system in France.

We get many foreign visitors at the Moscow Choreographic School. Some are statesmen and celebrities from various countries, and, of course, there are representatives of the arts. We have received Gerard Philippe and Marlene Dietrich, Albert Kahn and Solomon Hurok, Arnold Haskell and members of every ballet company to tour the USSR. The great ballet-masters and dancers Serge Lifar, Roland Petit, Ninette de Valois, Jerome Robbins, Robert Joffrey, Yvette Chauvire, Alicia Alonso, Leonid Massine, Maurice Bejart, Maria Tallchief, Marcia Haydée and many, many others have all been to see us.

George Balanchine was here in 1973 and wrote in our Visitors' Book: "Best wishes to your great school. My tradition comes from there too."

The School has a Museum attached to it. The permanent display tells of the School's history, famous former students, teachers and arrangements. The archives of the museum are most interesting, for they present information on and photographs of the students from the beginning of their studies in the first grade through their professional careers in theater companies.

In three to five minutes you can discover who graduated from the School in what year, which teachers they had, what roles they danced and who they went on to be. You will find a photo of the charming Katya Maksimova in the first grade, of the poetic Natalya Bessmertnova in the children's pas de trois in the 4th grade, or of the young Vladimir Vassiliev dancing in the graduation examination.

Thanks to our collection of classical dance lessons, you can learn how teachers 30-50 years ago conducted classes and compare their methods with contemporary ones.

The exquisite, ethereal profession of ballet requires of the children immense commitment, endurance and a real calling.

Our students do not have much spare time, and yet, surprisingly, in their leisure hours they are not at rest. On the contrary, they are constantly active.

There is no way one can develop a creative being and bring out personality without freedom for self-expression. We endeavor to make conditions which enable the students to express their ideas through dance.

In the first grades we leave time during the classical dance lessons for improvisation. The students often present individual etudes at acting classes.

We have a special performance for the graduating students in which many of the pieces are choreographed by the children themselves.

There is no end to the imagination of our students. We have found that our future dancers are also adept at drawing and singing.

They enjoy performing for amateur shows for their teachers. They spend long hours of secret preparation, writing scripts, arranging dances, learning the songs, words and movements of the drama and the mime scenes, and creating the costumes. They themselves select and perform the music.

It has become a tradition for the School to have "Festival of Arts," "Song Holiday," and "Boarding Birthday" shows and they are very popular events. What a collection of young talent! We have our very own jazz group and are forever arranging competitions and quizzes, meetings with famous actors, musicians, artists and students of other schools, excursions to museums and theaters, and discussions of what we have experienced.

Each winter the students have a break near Zvenigorod, a lovely place not far from Moscow. The skiing excursions and amateur song and drama competitions there make these holidays memorable.

The School garden and yard are a mass of greenery and flowers. The children plant them and look after them. The garden is always full of laughter. You hear the noise as the children play their games; some of them even play football. There in the playground our children are just like any others. But turn on the music and they become little theater artists. Their dream is to perform on the stage where the older students study and rehearse.

The pride of the School is the children's theater which has a stage nearly the size of the Bolshoi's. There is room for an audience of 500. Here we put on shows and concerts for Moscow's school and university students. Here we receive the School's honored guests.

The State Examinations take place on this stage. The classical dance exams start things off in a heightened mood of artistic endeavor. On the second day come the examinations on character dance. The audience is made up of ballet-masters, teachers, rehearsal instructors, and dancers from the various Moscow and other national ballet schools. For many years now the State Adjudication Panel has been chaired by Yuri Nikolaevich Grigorovich. I might just mention that his inspired ballets have a great impact on the process of choreographic education.

The school and the theater are a single whole. The ballet theater repertoire determines the work of the school and at the same time the theater repertoire is determined by the level of the professional aptitude of the graduates of the choreographic school.

It has become a firm tradition for the School to present a graduation concert at the end of each academic year at the Bolshoi Theater.

This is a true festival of the choreographic arts, a great event for the entire School, for all who took part in the instruction of the students from the 1st grade.

Each graduation performance has a flavor all its own. This is because each graduate gets special treatment at the School. Their vocational training is tailored to their individual creativity.

The graduation performance, something we prepare with great care is, in effect, the final examination for our pupils. With it they say farewell to the School and move away from friends and teachers.

That is the day the student turns into a true ballet performer, the day his or her professional life begins.

Then, our pupils, like swallows in spring, fly off to the ballet companies in all parts of our land.

Yet many are to be seen the next September 1 in the schoolyard. September 1 is a big day. Teachers and pupils—past and present—all gather in the yard with flowers. It is a sea of flowers and smiles. The graduates, already fully-fledged performers, present the little ones ballet shoes. What joy and happiness shines in the eyes of those first-graders! How many fine and happy moments they will enjoy and what a lot of tears there will be before their own graduation eight years later, where they give out tiny ballet shoes to a new generation of the School.

In recent years, classical dance has formed the backbone of the Graduation Show program. Performances of such pieces as an act from L. Minkus's "Paquita," S. Prokofiev's "Classical Symphony" or the second act of Tchaikovsky's "Swan Lake" convey a high level of professional aptitude.

In addition, we include variations and duets from classical ballets in the show program.

We also place major emphasis on national and folk dances solo and mass—Russian, Ukrainian, Spanish, Georgian and so on.

The pieces set to the music of modern composers are also very successful.

We teachers give our all to the students. For me, the School has become a home into which I invest all my strength and knowledge, all the fire in my soul. The demands of the contemporary ballet force me to constantly search and invent, and not to rest on my laurels. My life would not possess joy and purpose were I not an instructor in classical dance. For many of us teachers at the School, we extend our time on stage through our pupils.

From the School there have emerged such world-renowned dance stars as Plisetskaya, Liepa, Vassiliev, Maksimova, and Fadeechev.

My destiny as teacher and School Director is bound to the next generation, to names like Bessmertnova, Lavrovsky, Sorokina, Vladimirov, Golikova, Akimov, Leonova, Gordeeva, Bogatyrova, Drozdova, Tedeeva and Mikhalchenko.

My prime pupil was Natalya Bessmertnova. She immediately caught the eye. She was slim and delicate and had an extraordinary beauty and long smooth bodylines. The eyes were big and round, ever so serious and just a little sad. You could feel enormous talent in her and this at once gladdened and frightened. It is very important to comprehend a rare gift and channel it properly. One must cautiously and sparingly draw on such a talent.

Natalya was a favorite pupil of mine—very hard-working and willing to please, and quick to learn. At classes and rehearsals her alert eyes never left me.

In the final grade she represented our School at the Parma Festival in Italy.

She danced Saint-Saens "Dying Swan" and an adagio from "Swan Lake" and was immediately recognized as a star. The Italian press raved: "Bessmertnova possesses a softness and expressiveness of movement and sense of tender narration that, in combination with technique that can be called perfection, make her stand out clearly and even today promise her a big future."

Within a week of graduation, she was debuting with the Bolshoi Ballet in "Chopiniana," performing the mazurka and waltz. The hall was full of talk of an amazing new dancer of the romantic style. Her first performance of "Giselle" is totally unforgettable. The entire audience, and all the dancers and everyone behind the scenes was spellbound. It was a miraculous portayal!

Yuri Grigorovich took over the direction and training of Natalya Bessmertnova. And it has been a rare alliance of a highly talented ballet-master and an extremely gifted ballet-dancer.

Natalya Bessmertnova has become one of the greatest ballerinas of our time, the very pride of Soviet ballet-dancing.

I try never to miss one of her performances. After the performance I usually meet with her to comment. She listens with great care to my remarks. We have built up over the years a marvellous human and professional friendship.

I follow my other former pupils with great excitement too—for example, M. Leonova, A. Mikhalchenko, G. Stepanenko and O. Suvorova. What a source of happiness they are for me!

The life of the School is complex and diverse. Today, when one enters that bright palace of the arts, one invariably senses the fast rhythm of the classes, lectures and rehearsals. It is a rhythm pumping fresh strength, beauty and youth into Soviet ballet.

People's Artist of the USSR S.N. Golovkina,
A State Prize Winner

The Moscow Ballet Academy is the official name, but the whole world knows it as the "Bolshoi Ballet School." This is the prestigious, modern building which houses the school in Moscow.

Before a student is enrolled at the Academy a series of physical tests are performed before a faculty committee, including medical doctors who are familiar with the orthopedic aspects of dancing and are able to forecast physical problems.

The rigors of the physical examination are an annual episode. The children take it as a matter of course. They do not seem overly upset by the examination; "bored" might be a better word for it!

The physical examination can be quite extensive as almost every part of the child's body, as it pertains to dancing, is examined. The children who eventually graduate from the Academy are sent to the Bolshoi and other ballet companies all over the vast Soviet Union.

The three-stage examination for entrance to the School consists of (1) physique, beauty and body proportions; (2) a rigorous medical examination for defects which may be present or latent; (3) a panel of experienced teachers who judge the children's potential in dancing, acting, rhythm and coordination.

The children begin an eight year program. Their education will be complete, with lessons in political history, language, chemistry, mathematics, and almost every kind of dance suitable for the theater.

The photos on this page are actual candid photographs of the first class, that is, the students during their first year at the Academy.

The students at the Academy spend most of their time in school. They are taken from their homes and eat and live at the school. They are taught everything, including personal hygiene, that they might learn in a normal school education plus what parents are supposed to teach them.

More than 20 aspirants apply for each place. Only 90 children are accepted in any one year: 45 boys and 45 girls. The children must be ten years old and pass a very severe three-stage entrance examination.

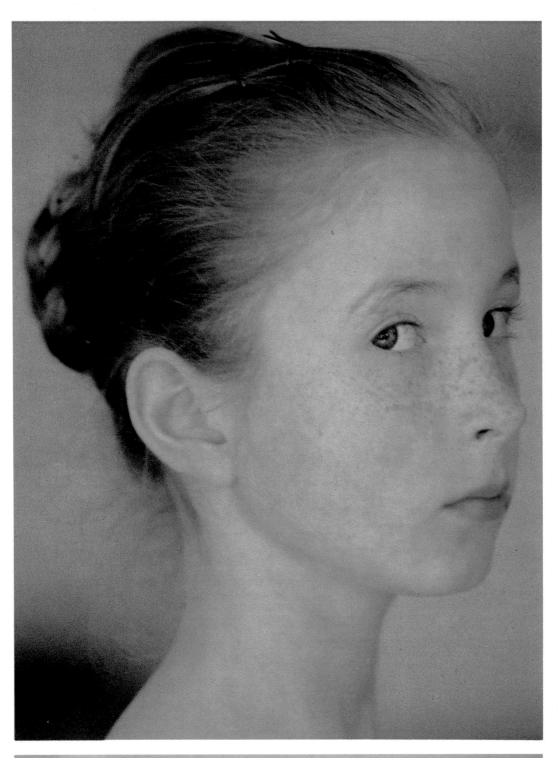

Children who have just
entered the Academy.
Beauty, dignity and grace
are already part of their
characters.

Did you ever see a youngster more proud or more secure? Is she destined to be a star?

The Soviet Union is a nation of song and dance. Almost every student in every school in the Soviet Union participates in singing, dancing, gymnastics or ice skating as well as every other popular sport.

Young boys, in their first term, being taught classical dance.

The ballet teachers travel the entire Soviet Union seeking talented youngsters. The School sees as its mission not only the training of highly professional ballet dancers, but artistically oriented graduates who will enter the general cultural scene as artists, writers, critics, historians, poets, etc.

The same dance but performed by second year students.

Classical dance second form, boys only.

The children have a gruelling schedule, being completely occupied from 9 A.M. to 6 P.M.

Classical dance is started from the first term, as soon as the child enters the School.

Boys in the first term gathering before a lesson.

Girls study without boys in the early years of their training.

A young boy eager to
start on his first day
in the school.

Each year the dance
curriculum changes,
gradually becoming more
difficult. Classical dance is
basic since it makes the
ballet dancer versatile by
promoting harmony,
coordination, expression,
stamina and technique. Even
the young children appear
extremely fit physically . . .
no one is overweight or
underweight.

Strict attention and strict
discipline are absolutely
demanded of all students in
the Bolshoi Academy.

The beautiful, talented O. Coval, a fifth year student.

To learn the skills necessary for successful ballet dancing, such courses as Classical, character Duet, Old Time and Modern dancing are given. This, in addition to seven years of piano lessons, history of ballet, theater, the arts and esthetics. The body, as well as the mind, is completely trained.

Warming up before the lesson is part of the physical routine taught the students.

33

The Soviet Union boasts of at least 60 opera and ballet companies . . . that's correct, opera AND ballet . . . both. The Moscow and Kirov Ballets also have their own opera companies . . . there is a Bolshoi Opera and a Kirov Opera!

Even their students begin to become recognizable as ballet dancers as these photos illustrate.

One of the senior students, A. Nikonov. (Below, left) Nikonov training with other boys in his class.

The Bolshoi School is huge. It has 20 large, bright-with-sunlight dance halls. On one wall, huge windows let in the sunlight; the opposite wall is mirrored. The floor is made of special pine . . . the kind previously used for the large sailing ships . . . the kind that absorbs shock well.

Classical dance training.

Senior girls at the classical dance class.

(Below) Maxim Martirosian, the artistic director of the School, is also a great teacher.

Male students in their seventh year at the Moscow Bolshoi Academy are expected to show exceptional talent. This is the next to last term and they are carefully instructed by teachers such as V. Koshelev, shown in the photo above. As the grades get higher, the students become fewer due to "wash-outs."

(Above) One of the great teachers at the school is Pyotr (Peter) Pestov. He is intensely interested in each and every student. He is an accomplished dancer himself and he keeps himself fit (right) by practicing with the students. This "togetherness" is an invaluable student aid.

Seven boys in the seventh form begin to show promise. At this stage it is easy to separate the mediocre from the great.

In addition to the 20 dance halls there are 20 music rooms where each student receives individual lessons. In many of the group lessons, older children help younger children. The older children are assigned, one on one, to help their younger colleagues. Not only is this helpful to the younger dancer, but it gives them all a basic training in teaching dance and enables them to see flaws which they might not notice if they worked alone.

Second form students helping their schoolmates. The Soviet Union is so large it encompasses many "nationalities." This young lady obviously comes from the southeast part of the Soviet Union.

Assisting your fellow student is part of the education. These are second form students.

Because the physical demands are so intense and muscles must develop properly, older students often work very closely together, discussing special problems with both their younger and older colleagues.

The fourth year dancers training in character dancing.

These two photos give some idea of the dedicated talent demonstrated by these young girls in the fourth term. Spanish dancing is being taught at this lesson.

Character dances from Russia, Hungary, Spain, Italy, Poland and the Ukraine are taught from the fourth year (age 14) through graduation. The style of the dance as well as the character and technique are very important. This school has a kind of internationalism in dance form.

The symmetry and uniformity of training comes from serious repetition under skillful guidance of the exceptional staff of the school.

One of the strengths of the School is to maintain the best traditions of classical dance while keeping apace of contemporary ballet repertoires.

The duet dance being taught at the seventh form.

During the last three years of study, ages 16, 17 and 18, students are taught duet dancing and acting. Every major ballet has a famous adagio (slow dance form). *Swan Lake, The Sleeping Beauty,* and *Giselle,* just to mention a few, are part of the standard duet curriculum at The Moscow Choreographic School (Bolshoi Ballet School).

The pas-de-deux performed by sixth year students, one year younger than those shown above.

41

Pas-de-deux performed by students in their seventh term.

Duet classes start when the students are 15 or 16 years old and are physically and professionally prepared for it. During their duet lessons the students first learn duet technique before beginning the short etudes invented by their duet instructor. They must wait for their final years before they actually learn adagio repertoire.

"Live music" from the piano is used in all classes. These second term students are practicing classical dance.

The author teaching classical dance to her seventh term girls.

The Bolshoi School is a training center for choreographic education where teacher training courses offer both theoretical and practical dance studies. All teachers have the same lesson plans and methods of teaching.

The success of a teacher depends upon contact and communication. Madame Golovkina teaches some advanced students.

Madame Golovkina in action. Not only does she run the largest and most successful ballet school in the world, but she also teaches. She is shown here teaching classical dance.

Classical dance lesson for third graders, by teacher N. Yashchenkova.

Teachers from the Bolshoi Ballet School dispense a great deal of advice and recommendations to associated schools throughout the Soviet Union. They travel extensively to give training and practical assistance. All are thoroughly trained dancers and teachers of the dance.

Teacher S. Mubaryakova explains an exercise to her first grade students.

44

Teacher A. Prokofiev giving a lesson in classical dance to his sixth grade students.

At the end of every year (the school year runs from the fall to the beginning of the summer), the students are evaluated in all the dance disciplines. The examination covers all the material in the curriculum for that year. These examinations are as much a test of the teachers' skills as they are of the students' ability to understand and follow the teachers' directions.

These three views show the hallway outside the classroom during the hourly break.

Break-time!

The Bolshoi Ballet School is located in central Moscow, along the beautiful Moscow River, with a shaded garden. The children receive exactly the same basic education as any pre-university student in Moscow. Their secondary education includes all the sciences, histories of dance, music and art, language studies in foreign languages, and literature. Their academic education is an important part of their overall training since many of the students will not be dancers in the long run, but will form the elite cadre of artistically inclined and educated people who become teachers, artists, scholars, writers, poets, painters, and journalists.

Taking lessons in French. Languages are an important part of the students' general education. French is the official language of ballet, the way Italian is the official language of music.

Students at the library. Ballet students are extremely intelligent and are achievers in the academic sense.

Throughout their training, special talents are identified and cultivated. One of the common characteristics of all the students is their beauty or physical attractiveness. There are the "born actors" who thrive on attention; and the very shy who might require special attention.

The faces of the boys all vary . . . but they have one thing in common . . . they are all handsome with expressive faces.

Especially expressive is this young chap in the chemistry class.

These two photos show the students in the chemistry class of teacher T. Petrova. Biology is taught in the same room.

September First is a special day for the Bolshoi Ballet School. On that day, when everyone hopes for good weather, the schoolyard fills with people of all ages. For it is on this day that school starts and teachers and pupils, both past and present, all gather together in the yard for a nostalgic encounter. The graduates of the school respect a time-honored tradition of giving a pair of dancing shoes to a beginning, first-year student. Imagine the thrill of receiving a pair of ballet shoes from one of the famous dancers of the Bolshoi or Kirov! Eight years later . . . or even eighteen .. . . the same scene takes place . . . only the parts change. The children graduate after eight years at the school and are sent all over the Soviet Union AFTER the very best have been selected for the Bolshoi by Yuri Grigorovich.

49

During break time, when the weather permits, the young dancers flock outside to play games designed to foster teamwork.

Sports, social activities, camaraderie and fellowship are all part of the planned curriculum. In most cases, dancing classical ballet is a team effort, and the children are brought up with team spirit in their play activities as well as their dancing studies. Even when playing ping pong, normally a game for two or four people, others join in to act as judges and trainers.

Physically dangerous sports are not usually encouraged, nor are such muscle-building activities as weight-lifting, as these tend to develop the wrong kind of muscles, bodies and mentalities.

The boys are not discouraged from physical . . . even dangerous . . . sports such as European football (soccer) which is so popular throughout Europe.

Boy meets girl and the joy is obvious, isn't it? This is the sixth term when the children are about sixteen or seventeen years old. They are beginning their pas-de-deux training.

During each lesson, perhaps several times, one of the boys takes a water sprinkling can and wets the special wooden floor so it won't be slippery.

The staff of the School is composed of more than 300 teachers . . . that's one teacher for each two students. Each teacher is a first-rate dancer with extensive ballet experience. Many have retired from the Bolshoi itself; most have had training in teaching.

Talking during lessons is strictly forbidden, but during the break intimate conversations ensue with miniature romances developing. Most dancers eventually marry other dancers or musicians.

Final examinations on pas-de-deux. Examinations are taken very seriously by both students and faculty.

Behind the scenes at the pas-de-deux auditions.

The long-established ties with the Bolshoi Theatre are the prime impetus of the School. The stages of the Bolshoi Theatre as well as the Stanislavsky-Nemirovich-Danchenko Music Theater use the children in *The Sleeping Beauty, Nutcracker* and *Don Quixote.* These experiences are extremely important . . . can you imagine the feeling of dancing in the Bolshoi with its world-famous stars . . . and to a house that is always packed?

The seventh year students exhibiting their pas-de-deux skills.

Sometimes the exams produce tears. It's part of the training. Perfection is a goal of every professional. But it is rarely achieved on a consistent basis except for the superstars.

54

These photos show dramatic acting lessons by seventh term students.

Acting is a most important part of dancing; after all, dancing is basically acting. The students spend considerable time studying theater . . . especially acting.

Drama lessons take place constantly and performances are always in costume and with an audience of peers and teachers.

The ballets performed by the children are immensely popular. Many of the "greatest of the great" danced the children's parts when they themselves were young. Natalya Bessmertnova, prima ballerina of the Bolshoi recalls affectionately how she was awarded the role of Amur in the dream scene from *Don Quixote.* It was her first appearance at the Bolshoi and it will remain in her heart forever. "It really was like a fairy-tale dream," she recalls.

The School has 600 students; 300 live in dormitories in what is referred to as the "Boarding Section." These students come from various parts of the Soviet Union as well as from abroad.

Many students are used as part of the corps-de-ballet, or as part of the casual performers. They are entranced about working with the famous stars of the Bolshoi. These actual behind-the-scene photos demonstrate the intense devotion of the students to their art. It also shows the magnificent work of our photographer, Vladimir Pcholkin, who takes these photos without flash and who dedicates his time to ballet photography.

The students of the Bolshoi School participate in many of the ballets staged in Moscow. Only the best students are selected and they are so keenly interested in every aspect of what is happening that they never take their rest pauses, but instead observe the mature, great dancers that they themselves hope to be some day.

Dancers U. Lushina and A. Lapshin performing *Swan Devotion* composed by D. Evgenidze, with choreography by V. Bokadoro.

In May 1986 the premiere of *Timur and his Friends,* a children's ballet, was presented at the school. Yuri Grigorovich himself, the great principal ballet-master of the Bolshoi, even went to the school to help. The students danced with such fervor and showed such appreciation that new children's ballets are being planned.

The Spanish Trio composed by M. Berio and choreographed by M. Martirosian. The dancers are S. Martirosian, D. Mikchailov and V. Mikchailov.

58

A Ukrainian dance called *Semiora* danced by pupils of the graduating class. Choreography by V. Pobezhimov. The music is folk music.

The students adore performing in real ballets . . . costumed and with proper scenery. It opens up a whole new world . . . it is the "payoff" to many, many years of intense, gruelling training. The shows put on by the school are mainly group dances, both classical and popular. Jazz is extremely important in the curriculum.

The most gifted children get the leading roles and if they perform well they are almost assured of a role at a major theater.

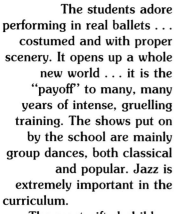

The Doll from *Coppelia.* The composer was Leo Delibes. The choreography was accomplished by A. Gorsky, S. Golovkina and M. Martirosian. The dancer is A. Nabokina, a fifth year student.

A Brazilian folk dance *At the Carnival* which was choreographed by N. Kumanina and performed by I. Grishina and A. Galkin.

Dancing duets is one of the highlights of the education of the dancers at the Bolshoi School. Modern, classical and nationalistic duets are daily reminders to the students of the many roles they must dance and the international and historical heritage they are preserving.

The pas-de-deux from *Coppelia* danced by A. Pestchanskaya and A. Lapshin. The composer was Leo Delibes with choreography by A. Gorsky, S. Golovkina and M. Martirosian. The dancers are seniors ready for graduation.

The pas-de-deux from *Timur and his Friends*. The music was composed by V. Agaphonnikov with choreography by A. Petrov. The dancers are N. Malandina and A. Petukov.

Mikhail Lavrosky dancing the role of the Nutcracker in Tchaikovsky's most popular ballet. Lavrosky is a highly decorated star having been awarded People's Artist of the USSR, Lenin Prize, State Prize of the USSR, Nezhinsky Prize of the Paris Academy of Dance, etc. He graduated from the Moscow Bolshoi Ballet School in 1961. His teacher was N. Tarasov.

61

The Bolshoi School prepares their own costumes. They are well made and very colorful as you can see.

To the right is the cast for *Timur and his Friends* composed by V. Agafonnikov with choreography by A. Petrov.

Alla Mikhalchenko dancing the role of Giselle in the ballet of the same name. She is an Honored Artist of the Uzbek SSR and a winner of international ballet competitions. She graduated from the School in 1975 and her teacher was the author, S. Golovkina. She is dancing with Alexei Phadeechev who is dancing Albert. He graduated in 1978 under A. Prokofiev.

Natalya Bessmertnova,
prima ballerina of Bolshoi
nowadays dancing the
leading role of Juliet in
Romeo and Juliet. She is
People's Artist of the USSR,
a Lenin Prize winner, winner
of the Anna Pavlova Prize of
the Paris Academy of Dance.
She graduated from Moscow
Ballet School in 1961 and
her teacher was S.
Golovkina.

Vijacheslav Gordeev dancing the role of Romeo in *Romeo and Juliet.* He is a People's Artist of the RSFSR, and a winner of international competitions. He graduated from the School in 1968 under the tutelage of P. Pestov.

Maya Plisetskaya as Isadora.
She is a People's Artist of the
USSR, a Lenin Prize winner.
Winner of the Anna Pavlova
Prize of the Paris Academy of
Dance, Hero of Labor, etc.
She graduated from the
Moscow Ballet School in
1943 and her teacher was E.
Gerdt.

Nina Ananiashvili dancing the role of Odette in *Swan Lake.* She is an Honored Artist of the RSFSR and a winner of competitions internationally. She graduated from the School in 1981. Her teacher was N. Zolotova.

Irek Mukhamedov dancing the role of Boris in Shostakovich's ballet *Golden Age.* He is an Honored Artist of the RFSFR and the winner of the Moscow Fourth International Competition. He graduated from the School in 1978 under the tutelage of A. Prokofiev.

Andris Liepa dancing the role of "Korsar." He is an Honored Artist of the RSFSR and a winner of competitions internationally (including Jackson in 1986). He graduated from the school in 1981.

Alexander Bogatyrev
dancing the role of Siegfried
in *Swan Lake.* He is a
People's Artist of the
RSFSR, a winner of
international competitions
and recipient of the
Nezhinsky Prize of the Paris
Academy of Dance. He
graduated from the Bolshoi
School in 1968. He studied
under P. Pestov.

69

Natalia Bessmertnova dancing the role of Anastasia in the ballet *Ivan the Terrible*. She is the prima ballerina of the Bolshoi and married to Yuri Grigorovich. She is universally acclaimed and her prizes include People's Artist of the USSR, Lenin Prize, Anna Pavlova Prize of the Paris Academy of Dance, etc. She graduated from the Bolshoi Ballet School in 1961 and was taught by the author, S. Golovkina. Yuri Vladimirov is dancing the role of Ivan. He is a People's Artist of the USSR, a winner of many international competitions, including the esteemed Nezhinsky Prize of the Paris Academy of Dance. He graduated from the Bolshoi School in 1962 and he studied with A. Ermolayev.

(Right) Ekaterina Maksimova dancing the role of Kitri in *Don Quixote*. She is a People's Artist of the USSR, a winner of the State Prize of the USSR and winner of international competitions including the coveted Anna Pavlova Prize at the Paris Academy of Dance. She graduated from the Bolshoi school in 1958 where she was taught by E. Gerdt.

Boris Akimov dancing the
role of Crassus in *Spartacus.*
He is a People's Artist of the
USSR, a winner of the State
Prize, a winner of
international competitions
and a graduate of the School
in 1965 when he studied
under M. Liepa.

The Bolshoi School prepares their own costumes. They are well made and very colorful as you can see.

Index